This scripture will always have thoughts of you attached, wonderful, loving thoughts.

Presented to

Moreen Froyum

On the occasion of

♥ "just because" ♥

From

Kristen L. Lincoln

Date

5/8/02

Thank you for helping me find my way to the cleft of the rock. (& the closet of Love)

Published by Barbour Publishing, Inc., P. O. Box 719, Uhrichsville, Ohio 44683
http://www.barbourbooks.com

 Member of the
Evangelical Christian
Publishers Association

Printed in China.

THOSE WHO HOPE IN THE LORD WILL

Soar As the Eagle

Sheryl Lynn Hill

BARBOUR
PUBLISHING, INC.

But they that wait upon the LORD
shall renew their strength;
they shall mount up with wings as eagles;
they shall run, and not be weary;
and they shall walk, and not faint.

ISAIAH 40:31 KJV

$\mathcal{S}$o God created. . .every winged bird according to its kind.
And God saw that it was good.

Like Eagles

What is an eagle? An eagle is strong, confident, and a devoted mate. It understands the thermal currents and uses them to spread its wings, soaring high above perilous storms. It uses the updrafts produced by rough terrain to help it fly with little effort. An eagle dwells on top of rocks and in the clefts of high places for protection. In the Bible those who trust in the Lord are likened to eagles, soaring majestically through life.

. . . .

God created us with an overwhelming desire to soar. . . . He designed us to be tremendously productive and "to mount up with wings like eagles," realistically dreaming of what He can do with our potential.

CAROL KENT

Waiting

Waiting is one of the hardest things to do, especially when the years go by and our dreams and plans have not yet been fulfilled. Indeed, we spend much of our lives waiting for direction.

The American Heritage Dictionary offers this definition of wait: "To remain inactive or stay in one spot until something anticipated occurs or to be in a state of readiness." Surely that describes the eagle, for it knows how to wait in many situations.

The eagle will perch on a rock waiting for the sun to rise and the wind to make thermal currents. While the eagle waits, it looks down to the ground to see if there is any prey. When it spots its prey, the eagle usually chooses to wait. Then, at the right moment, it swoops down.

Before we mount up on wings like eagles, we must learn to wait.

That was a lesson for the children of Israel who were told to wait for the cloud to guide them by day. They had to move when the cloud moved and wait when the cloud stopped.

Like the Old Testament Hebrews, occasionally we are told to wait in the midst of trials or heartache as "the cloud" disappears. Waiting can be for a few minutes or for many years.

Then there are times when we feel comfortable and settled into a place and we notice the cloud begins to move. When we move as God's hand guides us, safely under His wings, we will soar to new places and heights.

He will cover you with his feathers,
and under his wings you will find refuge;
his faithfulness will be
your shield and rampart.

PSALM 91:4 NIV

Under His wings I am safely abiding;
Tho' the night deepens and tempests are wild,
Still I can trust Him; I know He will keep me;
He has redeemed me, and I am His child.

Under His wings, under His wings,
Who from His love can sever?
Under His wings my soul shall abide,
Safely abide for ever.

William O. Cushing

. . . .

Be not dismayed whate'er betide,
God will take care of you;
Beneath His wings of love abide,
God will take care of you.

CIVILLA D. MARTIN

One of the first rules of aerodynamics is that flying into the wind quickly increases altitude. The wings of the airplane create more lift by flying against the wind. How was this lesson learned? It was learned by watching birds fly. If a bird is simply flying for pleasure, it flies with the wind. But if it senses danger, it turns into the wind to gain altitude and flies up toward the sun.

MRS. CHARLES E. COWMAN
Streams in the Desert

. . .like an eagle that stirs up its nest and hovers over its young,
that spreads its wings to catch them
and carries them on its pinions.

DEUTERONOMY 32:11 NIV

. . . .

Herein is love:

When I cannot rise to Him,

He draws near on wings of grace,

to raise me to Himself.

PURITAN PRAYER

On the Wings of an Eagle

An eagle's wings are long and wide, helping it to soar skillfully through the sky. The primaries, on the tip of the wings, are tapered so that the eagle can fully expand its wings and separate them widely. Such a design reduces turbulence as the air passes smoothly over its wings.

The eagle does not flap its wings; it soars! Unlike a duck, which will frantically flap its wings at the first sign of trouble, making it vulnerable to predators, the eagle conserves its energy, trusting in its God-given strength.

We can be like eagles as we soar on the wings of God.

. . . .

I can face that which I must endure while in my Father's arms.

MIRIAM BROWN

If I go up to the heavens, you are there;
if I make my bed in the depths, you are there.
If I rise on the wings of the dawn,
if I settle on the far side of the sea,
even there your hand will guide me,
your right hand will hold me fast.

PSALM 139: 8–10 NIV

. . . .

Go out into the darkness
and put your hand into the Hand of God.
That shall be to you better light
and safer than a known way.

MINNIE LOUISE HASKINS

Soaring to New Places

When my husband retired from his job, to me that meant it was time to move. For the past several years we had been living in northern California, but now, as my husband ended his career, we were all set to move closer to family in Michigan, with bank accounts started and a small apartment picked out.

Then my husband received another job offer, also in California, but one that would require a different move. As he seemed determined to take the job, I began pouring my heart out to God.

In my daily devotionals, I came upon the passage in the Book of Ruth where Boaz comforts Ruth: " I've been told all about what you have done for your mother-in-law since the death of your husband—how you left your father and mother and your homeland and came to live with a people you did not know before. May the LORD repay you for what you have done. May you be richly rewarded by the LORD, the God of Israel, under whose wings you have come to take refuge" (Ruth 2:11–12, NIV).

As I thought about that passage, I knew God was reassuring me not to look back where I had come from, but to look forward to our new home. God knew what I was giving up, but He had something better in mind. He wanted me to rest under the shelter of His wings and take refuge in Him.

> *May* you grow to be beautiful
> as God meant you to be
> when He first thought of you.
> AUTHOR UNKNOWN

. . . .

The Eagle

One spring day a boy was playing in the woods when suddenly he spotted something that looked like a nest. As he crept closer he saw it was a bird's nest with only one egg in it. Instinctively, he looked around but he didn't see any birds flying above him. The boy decided to take the egg home.

After showing the egg to his parents, he placed it in the chicken coop. (He hoped a chicken would sit on the egg until it hatched.) Finally, the day came for the hatching, and excitedly the boy ran and got his parents to come see the baby bird. But then came the revelation: The boy's father looked at the baby bird and told his son it was an eagle.

As the eagle grew, the boy's father helped clip its wings. The eagle seemed content in the barnyard with all the chickens.

Summer came, and the boy and his father became busy and

forgot about the eagle. The father forgot to keep the eagle's wings clipped. No one noticed that the eagle grew more restless with each passing day.

With the change of seasons, it was inevitable that a summer storm would come, too. As the wind moaned and whipped through the barnyard, all the chickens began to hurry and scurry to find shelter. But not the eagle. The eagle stood with its wings spread out, looking into the sky. There, amid the pelting rain and lightning flashes was another eagle soaring with the storm.

Just then a gust of wind arose. The wind filled the young eagle's wings, enabling it to lift up from the ground and soar high into the sky with the other eagle. At last, soaring with another eagle, the orphaned bird knew its purpose in life.

Like the eagle, we too can learn our purpose in life once we know the great love our heavenly Father has for us.

. . . .

*How great is the love
the Father has lavished on us,
that we should be called children of God!
And that is what we are!*

1 JOHN 3:1 NIV

I lift up my eyes to the hills—
where does my help come from?
My help comes from the LORD,
the Maker of heaven and earth.

PSALM 121:1–2 NIV

> *he eagle that soars in the upper air*
> *does not worry itself how it is to cross rivers.*
> GLADYS AYLWARD

. . . .

Eagle Vision

Eagles are noted for their exceptionally keen eyesight. An eagle's eyes can see both straight ahead and to the side simultaneously.

This remarkable skill serves the eagle well as it flies high in the sky to seek out its prey. The majestic bird has been known to see fish from several hundred feet above the water.

Helen Keller, the American writer and lecturer who was blind from birth, wrote: "To have eyes and no vision would be worse than being blind." Yet how many times am I soaring blindly when I have forgotten to look for God and His strength to guide me!

In the Bible, Lot's wife used her eyes but not her vision. Going against what the angel of the Lord had instructed her to do, she looked back. Lot's wife may have been thinking of all the riches and comforts she was leaving behind, or maybe she just couldn't believe God would really destroy her home, the city of Sodom. Whatever her reason for looking back, she instantly became a pillar of salt.

God created us with eyes to see. We may not be able to see as the eagle does, both forward and to the side at the same time, but we can look to the hills, to the Lord, for strength. And, once seeing, we will have attained true "eagle vision."

. . . .

*Y*ou, my soul, have also experienced it. Aren't there times of deepest depression the moments that immediately follow your loftiest highs? Just yesterday you were soaring high in the heavens and singing in the radiance of the morning. Today, however, your wings are folded and your song is silent.

MRS. CHARLES E. COWMAN
Streams in the Desert

Renewal

To prepare for flight, the eagle spends an hour each day preening its feathers. Perched high on a rock, the eagle methodically passes each feather, up to 1200 in all, through its mouth and breathes on each one. This action produces a similar effect to steam cleaning. Once the feathers are restored, the eagle is ready to soar through the sky.

The eagle also has a gland that secretes an oily liquid, making its feathers waterproof. When it rains or the bird dives into water after prey, the eagle's feathers do not become heavy with water or endanger its ability to fly.

We, too, must renew ourselves daily before the Lord or we will become "grounded." Without those necessary "quiet times," cares and concerns bring on anxieties and fears that slow us down. Worry renders us powerless and our faith begins to falter. When we worry we take on burdens we were never meant to carry.

"Fretting springs from a determination to get our own way," said Oswald Chambers. "Our Lord never worried and He was never anxious, because He was not 'out' to realize his own ideas; he was 'out' to realize God's ideas. . . . Deliberately tell God that you will not fret about that thing. All our fret and worry is caused by calculating without God."

Worry comes from natural concerns that are part of our lives.

But when these legitimate concerns are handled wrongly, they dominate our lives. Worry can make us forget that our caring God is in control and cause us to wonder about our future, over which we have no control.

Renewing ourselves is a daily process, just as it is for the eagle. This prayer of Ruth Bell Graham is my prayer, too, when I have a day filled with worry. "Lord, when my soul is weary and my heart is tired and sore, and I have that failing feeling that I can't take it anymore; then let me know the freshening found in simple, child-like prayer, when the kneeling soul knows surely that a listening Lord is there."

Abba Father,
Your Word is so full of
Your wonderful promises to care for me.
They help me to relax in heart,
to live by faith and not by sight.

ANNE ORTLUND

$\mathcal{C}$onfident in herself and aware of her God-given strength . . .she enjoys an inner contentment that isn't based on accomplishments, status, authority, power, or other people's opinions. This woman of God has learned the value of being as opposed to doing.

AUTHOR UNKNOWN

. . . .

*. . .in quietness and confidence
shall be your strength.*

ISAIAH 30:15 NKJV

Eagle Confidence

After the first year, the eaglet becomes independent. It has good eyesight, its talons are sharp, and it can fly and find its own food. Newly confident, the young eagle no longer has to depend on its parents but on its own ability.

Like the eagle, we must remain confident in our God-given abilities and strengths rather than on what other people think or say about us. Yet we cannot be as totally independent as the eagle and soar on our own. As we find our quiet confidence in the Lord, we find our strength. This gives us true assurance.

Assurance is not based on our own abilities but rather, on the inward peace we get as we daily depend on God's grace and strength.

Confidence based on our own abilities or achievements is false.

. . . .

So do not throw away your confidence;
it will be richly rewarded.

HEBREWS 10:35 NIV

Getting Our Eagle Wings

There is a fable about the way birds first got their wings. The story goes that initially they were made without them. Then God made the wings, set them down before the wingless birds, and said to them, "Take up these burdens and carry them."

The birds had sweet voices for singing and lovely feathers that glistened in the sunshine, but they could not soar in the air. When asked to pick up the burdens that lay at their feet, they hesitated at first. Yet soon they obeyed, picked up the wings with their beaks, and set them on their shoulders to carry them.

For a short time the load seemed heavy and difficult to bear, but soon, as they continued to carry the burden and to fold the wings over their hearts, the wings grew attached to their little bodies. They quickly discovered how to use them and were lifted by the wings high into the air. The weights had become wings.

This is a parable for us. We are the wingless birds, and our duties and tasks are the wings God uses to lift us up and carry us heavenward. We look at our burdens and heavy loads, and try to run from them, but if we will carry them and tie them to our hearts, they will become wings. And on them we can then rise and soar toward God.

There is no burden so heavy that when lifted cheerfully with love in our hearts will not become a blessing to us. God intends for our tasks to be our helpers; to refuse to bend our shoulders to carry a load is to miss a new opportunity for growth.

J. R. MILLER
Streams in the Desert

*No matter how overwhelming,
any burden God has lovingly placed
with His own hands on our shoulders
is a blessing.*

FREDERICK WILLIAM FABER

. . . .

Cast all your anxiety on him
because he cares for you.
1 PETER 5:7 NIV

But flies an eagle flight, bold and forth on,
Leaving no tract behind. . . .

WILLIAM SHAKESPEARE

. . . .

Brethren, I count not myself to have apprehended: but this one thing I do, forgetting those things which are behind, and reaching for unto those things which are before, I press toward the mark for the prize of the high calling of God in Christ Jesus.
PHILIPPIANS 3:13–14 KJV

There are only two lasting bequests
we can hope to give our children.
One of these is roots;
the other, wings.

HODDING CARTER III

. . . .

A bird's egg comprises a wondrous balance. It bears the weight of an incubating parent, and yet is not so thick that the grown hatchling cannot get out.   MARYJO KOCK

27

The View from the Nest

Eagles build their nests high up on a cliff or in a tree. The nest can be huge, weighing as much as two tons, and spreading as big as twenty feet long and nine feet wide.

When the foundation of the nest is done, the female stops gathering the materials and stays home, putting the finishing touches on the nest. The male keeps bringing home vines, leaves, and fur from its prey.

The nest completed, the female then lays one to two eggs and plucks many feathers from her body to pad the nest for the eaglets. While she is busy keeping the eggs warm, the male goes out and finds food to bring home for her.

A devoted "father," the male eagle brings "toys" home for the baby eaglets. Tennis balls, cans, and even old shoes may be seen in many nests. When the nest becomes too cluttered, the female simply tosses out some of the items.

When it's time for the eaglets to leave the nest, all the toys and the feathers put there for padding are removed. Suddenly, the nest becomes uncomfortable as the birds sit on only branches and twigs.

When it's time to learn how to fly, the female picks an eaglet up in her mouth. She carries it high up into the air and then drops it. Then she catches the baby before it hits the ground. She repeats this process several times until the eaglet understands and starts to fly on its own.

Sometimes we get pushed out of our nests.

Sometimes we become so comfortable in our environment that we want to stay there forever. Yet the Lord gently removes us from our comfort zone and teaches us to fly on His wings of love and protection.

The view from the nest can look scary and full of many dangers. But once we let go and learn to fly we will never want to return.

. . . .

Once we've tasted being alive,
we can't go back to being dead.
Aliveness in God is addictive.

NANCY GROOM

But like thine own eagle
that soars to the sun. . .

LEONARD HEATH

. . . .

For the LORD God is a sun and shield; the LORD bestows favor and honor; no good thing does he withhold from those whose walk is blameless.　　　PSALM 84:11 NIV

Even in winter, even in the midst of the storm, the sun is still there. Somewhere, up above the clouds, it still shines and warms and pulls at the life buried deep inside the brown branches and frozen earth. The sun is there! Spring will come! The clouds cannot stay forever.

GLORIA GAITHER

. . . .

Soaring into the Sun

For many years the eagle was thought to be the only animal capable of looking directly into the sun.

Aristotle wrote that the eagle would test its eaglets by making them look directly at the sun. If an eaglet would not do this it would be rejected. The Aztecs believed the eagle would fly into the sun early in the morning to receive its strength. Myth had it that as the eagle grew old and its wings and eyes started to fail, it would fly in the sky and circle into the sun singeing, or burning, its wings as its vision was renewed.

Physically and spiritually, the sun is key to our lives as well. Without the sun, our planet would be frozen and barren. Furthermore, we have a promise in the Bible that while on earth "the Lord is a sun and shield to us." However, when we leave this earth and go to heaven, we will have no need for the sun: "The city [the new Jerusalem] does not need the sun or the moon to shine on it, for the glory of God gives it light. . ." (Revelation 21:23, NIV). When we reach our eternal home, God's glory will shine brighter than the sun.

. . . .

. . .and his throne
endure before me like the sun.

PSALM 89:36 NIV

. . . .

*M*ay God send His love like sunshine in His warm and gentle way, to fill each corner of your heart each moment of today.   AUTHOR UNKNOWN

*Then Jesus declared,
"I am the bread of life.
He who comes to me
will never go hungry,
and he who believes in me
will never be thirsty."*

JOHN 6:35 NIV

. . . .

*D*ear ones, let us be takers and feed on the words of Jesus, the Son of God, our living bread. His words lead us directly back to Him, the Redeemer and Savior of the world.　　　　　　　　　　　ROSALIND RINKER

Eagle Diet

Eagles prefer to eat live fish rather than dead fish. If eagles cannot find fresh fish, they have been known to eat ducks and other small animals.

We, too, thrive when we eat properly. If we eat right, we feel healthy and full of energy. If we eat the wrong foods, we tend to drag around and not feel quite like ourselves.

To sustain ourselves spiritually, we must feed on the living bread of life that comes from the Bible, the Word of God. The Lord promises we will never be hungry or thirsty if we eat the bread of life.

If my life is broken when given to Jesus, it is because pieces will feed a multitude, while a loaf will satisfy only one little lad.

ELISABETH ELLIOT

Running the race living for Christ
and growing into His image—
requires focus and discipline.

ELIZABETH GEORGE

. . . .

Running the Race

The prophet Isaiah tells us that we are to soar like eagles and to run and not grow faint. In Hebrews 12:1 (NIV) we are reminded, "Therefore, since we are surrounded by such a great cloud of witnesses, let us throw off everything that hinders and the sin that so easily entangles, and let us run with perseverance the race marked out for us."

We must not let anything distract us from our God-willed destinies. When unresolved issues, strained relationships, hurts from the past, and feelings of failure threaten to pull us down, let us claim the promises from God's Word and pray each day.

When we choose to let go, giving those hurts or disappointments to the Lord, we are free to soar like the mighty eagle.

My faith was tested daily,
and the only way to pass those tests was
by God's grace one day at a time.

ELIZABETH GEORGE

. . . .

Great faith is often built during great trials.

OUR DAILY BREAD

. . . .

Let us fix our eyes on Jesus,
the author and perfecter of our faith.

HEBREWS 12:2 NIV

Looking Back

The eagle deals with its survival one day at a time.

Looking back to our past can be helpful if we learn from our mistakes and failures. When we dwell in the past, however, we cause ourselves unnecessary frustration, becoming discouraged and possibly despondent. In the Book of Hebrews we are told to "fix our eyes on Jesus, the author and perfecter of our faith." Jesus is the source of our faith. He will be the one to perfect us.

We can trust God with our past, present, and future. The apostle Paul writes, "Being confident of this, that He who began a good work in you will carry it on to completion until the day of Christ Jesus" (Philippians 1:6, NIV).

We have God-confidence in knowing that the Lord makes us whole and complete in Him. Let us focus on these promises instead of looking over our shoulders to past regrets and failures. Let us soar like the eagle!

The LORD is my rock, my fortress and my deliverer; my God is my rock, in whom I take refuge. He is my shield and the horn of my salvation, my stronghold. PSALM 18:2 NIV

. . . .

I hold not the Rock, but the Rock holds me,

The Rock holds me. . .

I rest on the Rock, and the Rock holds me,

Resting on the Rock of God.

MRS. C. RICE

Living in the Cleft of a Rock

Some species of eagles live in the clefts of rocks. Such a refuge provides protection for the eagle and its young. Living on the rock allows the eagle to see for many miles at a time and to detect early the arrival of dangerous predators.

As we dwell in the Rock of our Lord, we are also prepared to face anything that comes our way. Yes, troubles come into everyone's lives. We can allow them to shape us and build our character, asking God for strength and wisdom, or we can allow them to shake up our world.

When my husband was once laid off from a job, my first impulse was to panic and fret. Then I remembered this promise from Psalm 27:5 (NIV): "For in the day of trouble he will keep me safe in his dwelling; he will hide me in the shelter of his tabernacle and set me high upon a rock."

At that moment I found peace in not allowing myself to dwell on all the anxious possibilities such a loss might entail. Knowing that I had to dwell on the Rock of Jesus Christ and let Him take care of the situation gave me peace.

We must remember that to dwell in the Rock of the Lord's protection, we must give up our limited understanding and trust Him totally. When we do this we will not be shaken.

But they that wait upon the LORD
shall renew their strength;
they shall mount up with wings as eagles;
they shall run, and not be weary;
and they shall walk, and not faint.

ISAIAH 40:31 KJV